# My RAINBOW ACTIVITY BIBLE

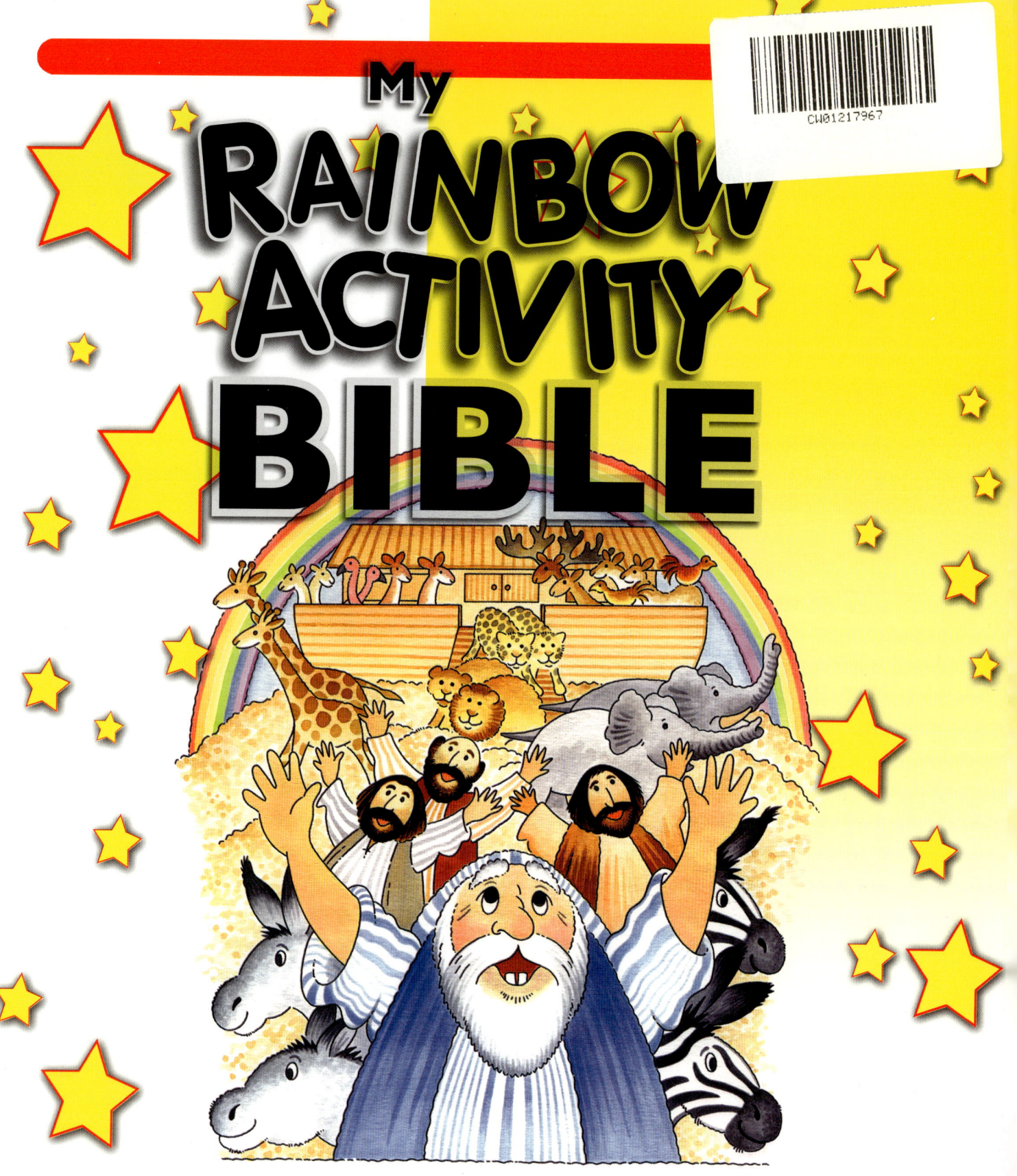

Bethan James and Gillian Chapman

# Noah builds an ark

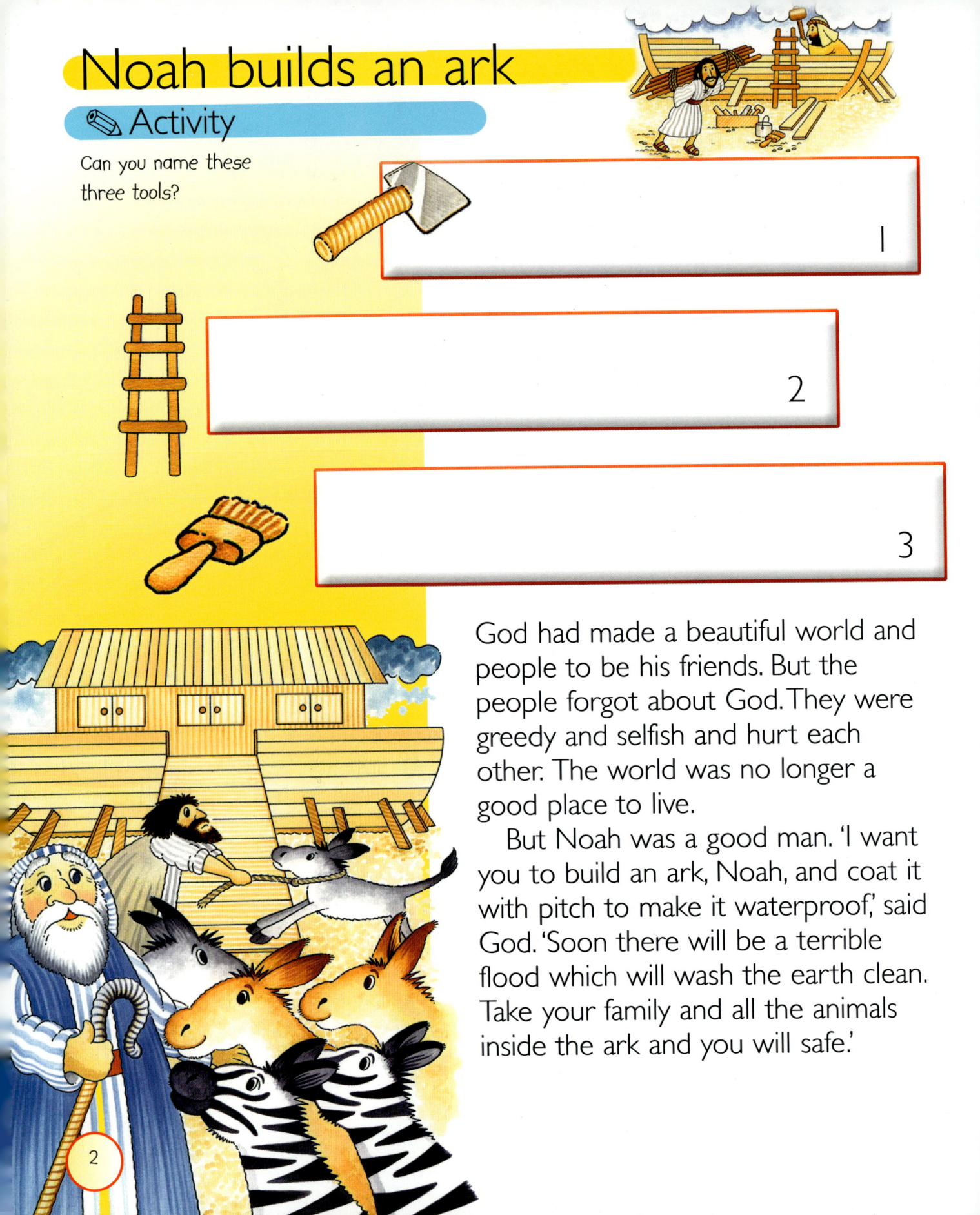

### ✏️ Activity

Can you name these three tools?

1.

2.

3.

God had made a beautiful world and people to be his friends. But the people forgot about God. They were greedy and selfish and hurt each other. The world was no longer a good place to live.

But Noah was a good man. 'I want you to build an ark, Noah, and coat it with pitch to make it waterproof,' said God. 'Soon there will be a terrible flood which will wash the earth clean. Take your family and all the animals inside the ark and you will safe.'

# Animals, two by two

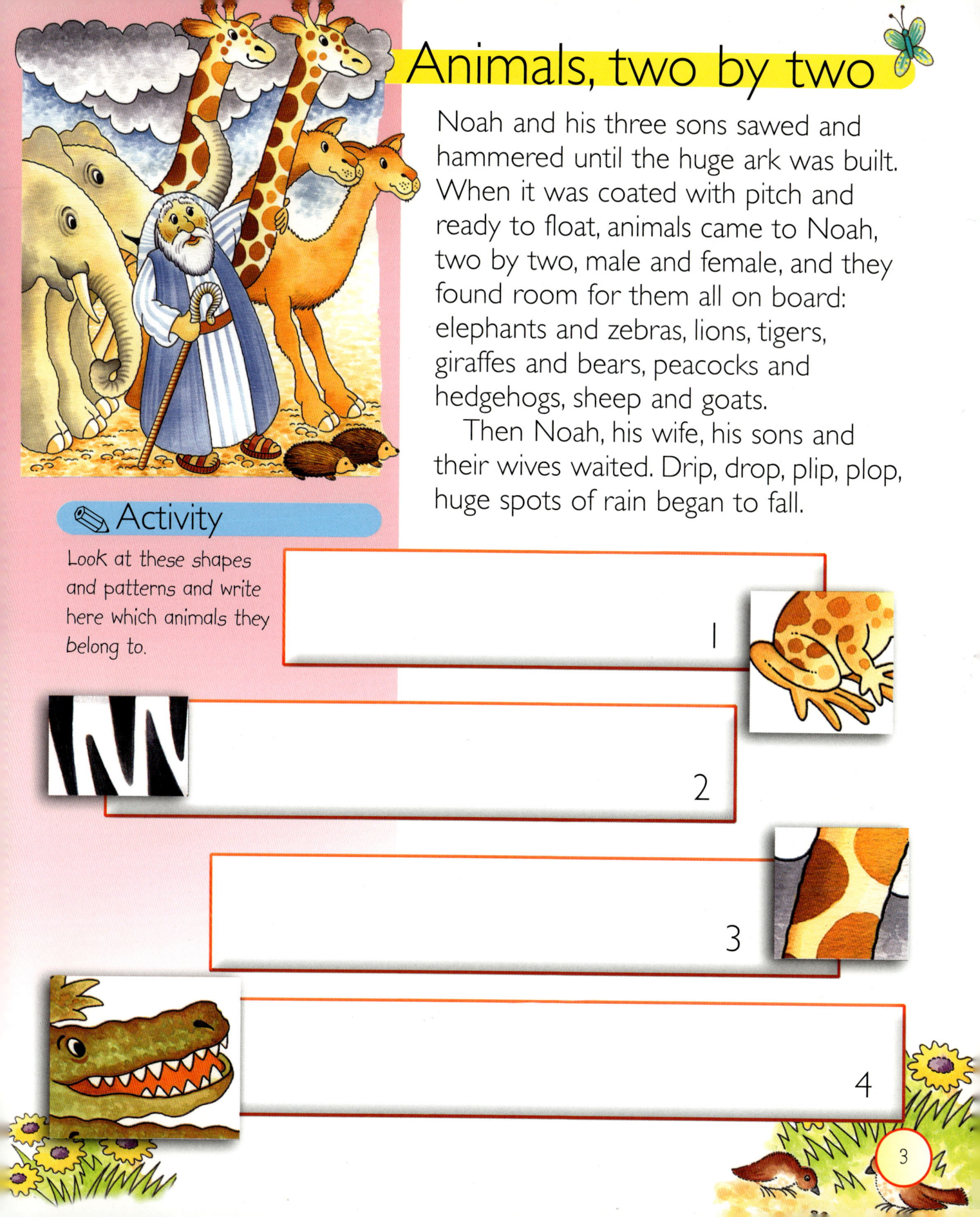

Noah and his three sons sawed and hammered until the huge ark was built. When it was coated with pitch and ready to float, animals came to Noah, two by two, male and female, and they found room for them all on board: elephants and zebras, lions, tigers, giraffes and bears, peacocks and hedgehogs, sheep and goats.

Then Noah, his wife, his sons and their wives waited. Drip, drop, plip, plop, huge spots of rain began to fall.

## ✏ Activity

Look at these shapes and patterns and write here which animals they belong to.

1.
2.
3.
4.

# The terrible flood

## ✏️ Activity

Complete the picture below by adding a few more waves.

It rained and it rained for forty days and forty nights. Streams became rivers and rivers became seas. Soon nothing could be seen but water.

Then one day the rain stopped. Everything was quiet – apart from the noisy animals on Noah's ark.

Then slowly, very slowly, the water went down until the tops of the trees could be seen again.

Noah sent out a raven, and later a dove. It was only when the dove brought back an olive leaf that Noah knew they would soon be able to leave the ark.

## ✏️ Activity

There are three different kinds of big cat in the picture. Write their names in the boxes.

1.
2.
3.

# The beautiful rainbow

The ark came to rest on Mount Ararat. When the door was opened the animals galloped and trotted and ran out into the new world outside.

The sheep had had lambs and the horses had had foals. They were all ready to start again.

### Activity
Complete the picture of the lion.

### Activity
Name these colours found in the rainbow.

R ___

O _____

Y _____

G ____

B ___

# Joseph's coat

Joseph was part of a large family. He had eleven brothers and one sister. But Joseph knew his father, Jacob, loved him best of all.

One day Jacob gave him a very special coat. Joseph's brothers were very jealous.

Then Joseph dreamed that one day he would be the greatest of all his family… His brothers were very cross. They didn't like Joseph at all.

## Activity

Joseph's coat was very colourful. What new colour do you make if you mix these colours?

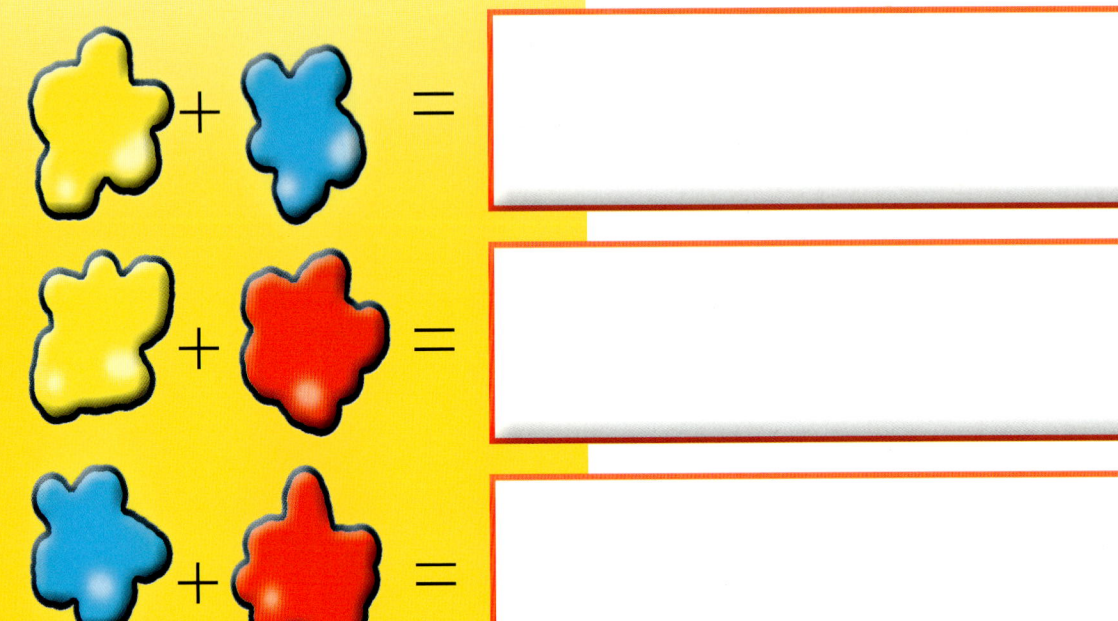

yellow + blue =  1

yellow + red =  2

blue + red =  3

# Sold to be a slave

Joseph's brothers began to plot against him. One day he came to see them while they were watching over their father's sheep. They took away his beautiful coat and sold him to some traders who were travelling to Egypt.

The brothers told Jacob that Joseph had been attacked and killed by a wild animal. Jacob thought he would never be happy again.

## Activity

Look at these two camels. Circle five differences between them.

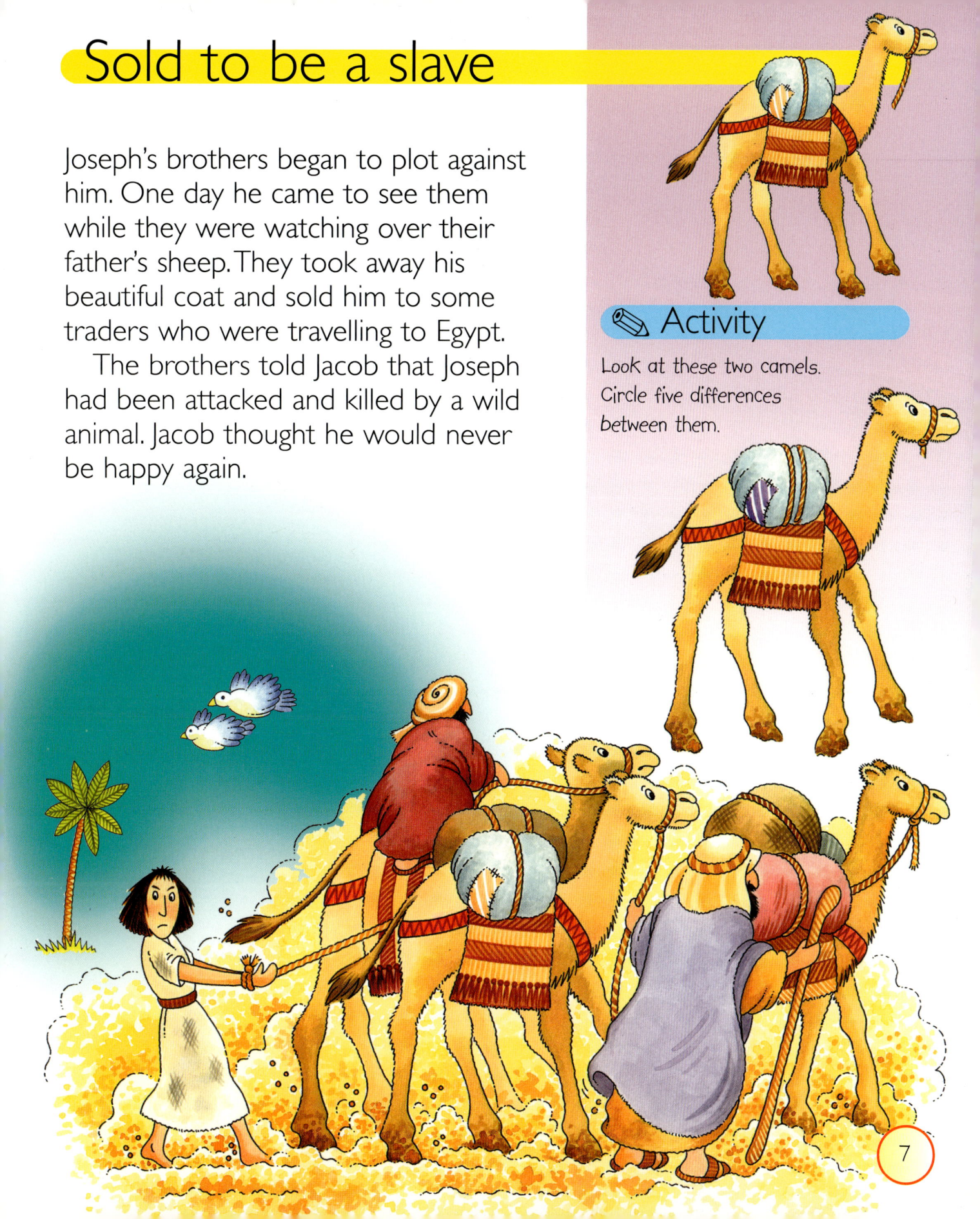

# Joseph goes to prison

Joseph was sold as a slave to Potiphar and he worked very hard in Egypt. But just as everything began to go right, it all went wrong and Joseph found himself in prison!

Joseph worked very hard in prison. When two of the king's servants joined him there, Joseph was even able to help them understand their dreams.

## Activity

Which prisoner is which? Write the answers above each prisoner:
'W' for wine steward,
'B' for baker and
'S' for shepherd.

# Dreams come true

### ✏️ Activity

Can you help Jacob find the way to Joseph?

Suddenly Joseph was a hero – and he began to understand that God had brought him to Egypt to save his people from the famine.

When he was released from prison, Joseph took care of all the grain that was grown in the country so no one went hungry. He forgave his brothers and brought his father and the whole family to live with him there.

# The baby in the basket

## ✏️ Activity

Can you find six differences between these two pictures? Draw a circle around them.

Many years later, the king of Egypt was very worried about the huge number of people who were descended from Joseph's family. First he made them his slaves. Then he decided to kill all their new baby boys.

Miriam's mother hid her baby son in a basket by the River Nile. When the princess came to the river, she saw the baby and wanted to keep him. She named him Moses.

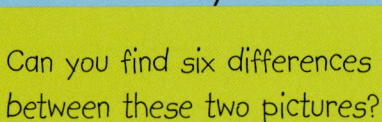

10

# The burning bush

When Moses was a man, he saw a slave being beaten. Moses killed the slave-driver to save the man, then he ran away into the desert to hide.

One day while he was watching over sheep, Moses saw a bush that seemed to be on fire but did not burn up. God spoke to Moses from the burning bush.

'Go to the king of Egypt, Moses. Tell him to let my people go.'

## Activity

Which shoe is the same style as the shoes in the picture?

A B C D E

## Activity

How many frogs can you find on these two pages?
Circle each frog and write the answer in the box.

# Ten terrible plagues

The king would NOT let God's people go.

God sent nine plagues to Egypt: the river turned to blood, there were frogs, gnats, flies, animal disease, boils, hail, locusts and deep darkness. Each time the king agreed to let his slaves go. But when God took the plague away, the king changed his mind.

God told his people to get ready for a journey because that night the angel of death would pass over them. When God sent the tenth plague, the king told Moses to take God's people – and GO!

## Activity

Tick (✓) the things that plagued the Egyptians and mark with a cross (✗) the things that were not plagues.

12

# Crossing the Red Sea

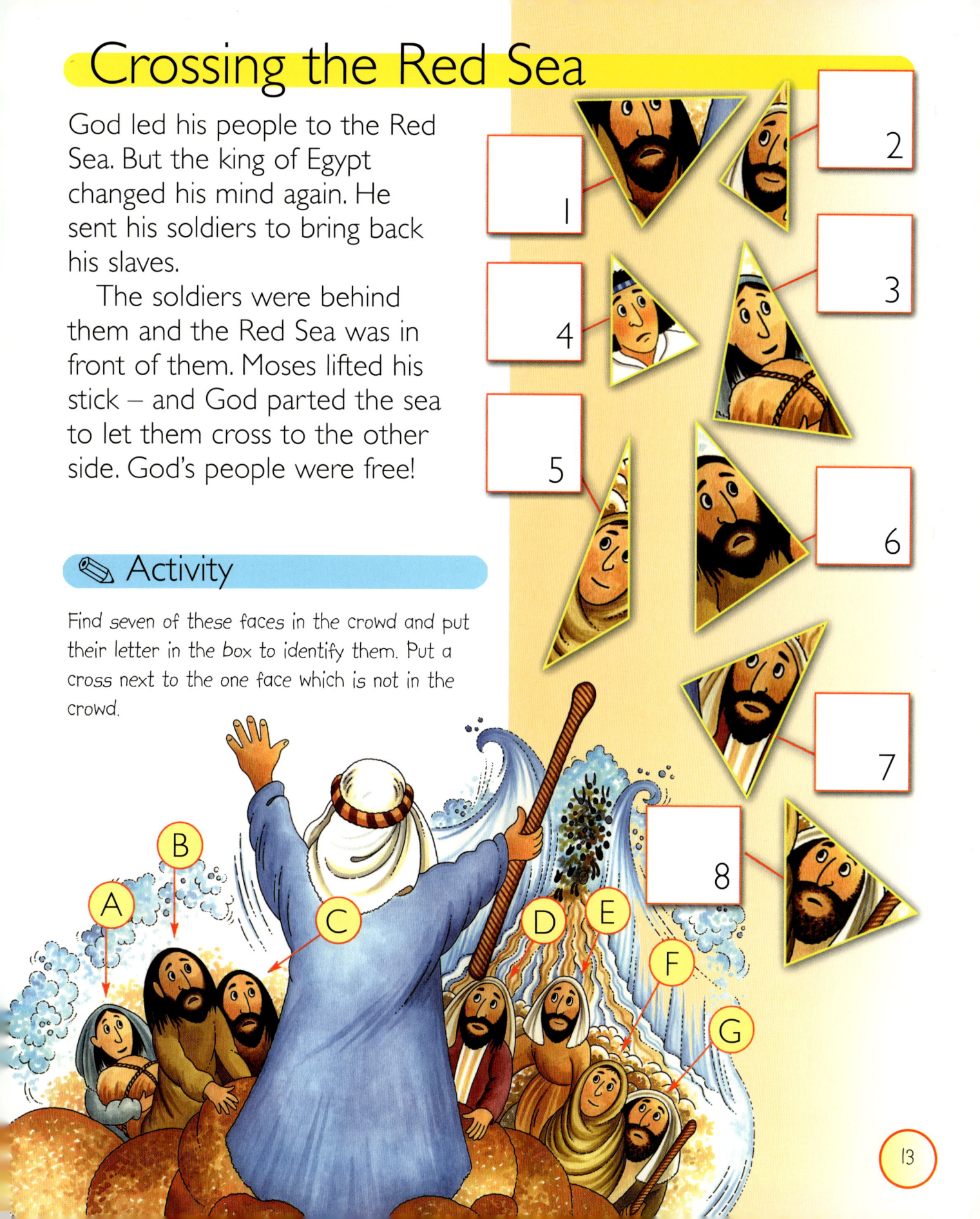

God led his people to the Red Sea. But the king of Egypt changed his mind again. He sent his soldiers to bring back his slaves.

The soldiers were behind them and the Red Sea was in front of them. Moses lifted his stick – and God parted the sea to let them cross to the other side. God's people were free!

## ✏️ Activity

Find seven of these faces in the crowd and put their letter in the box to identify them. Put a cross next to the one face which is not in the crowd.

13

# The ten commandments

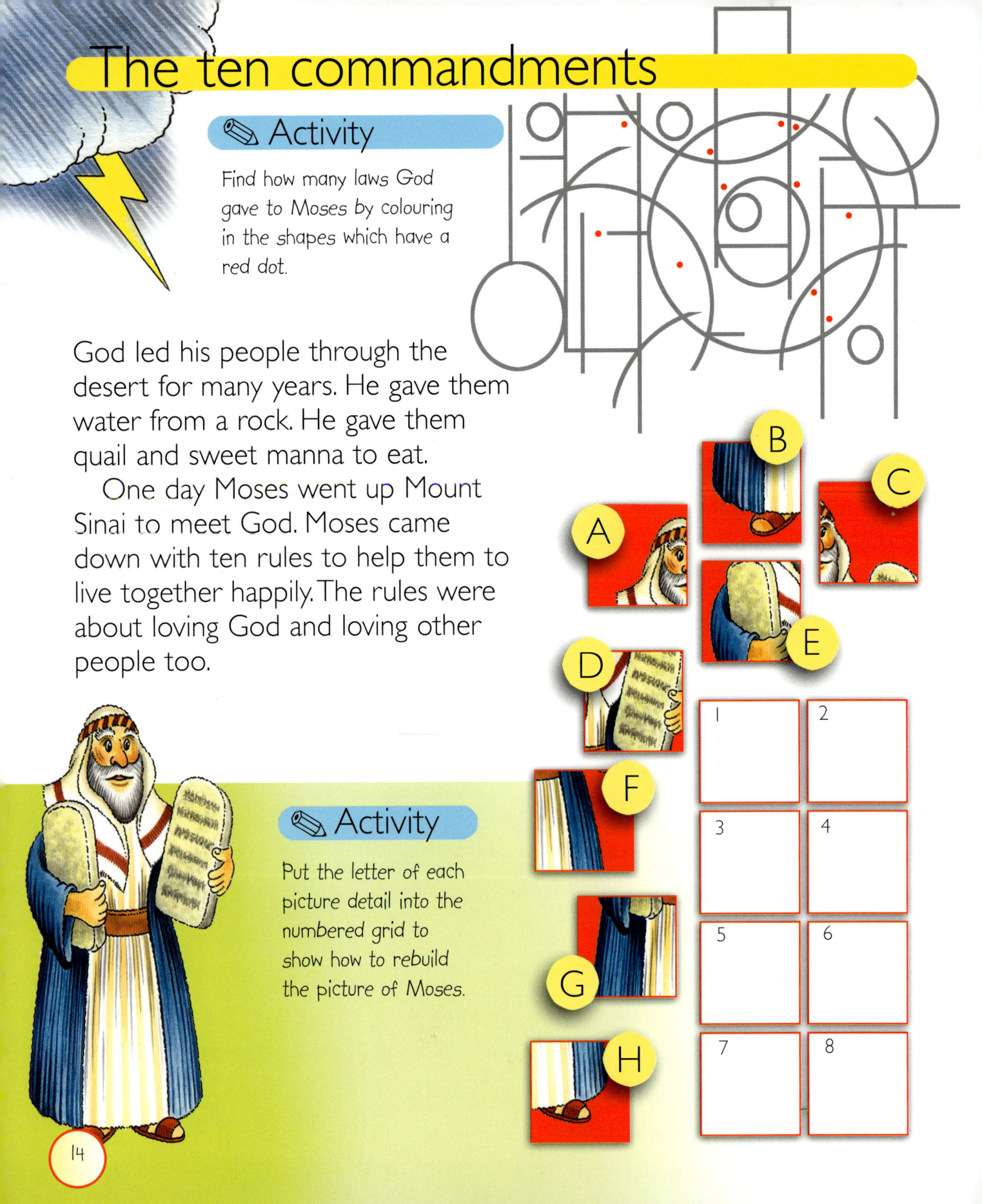

### ✏️ Activity

Find how many laws God gave to Moses by colouring in the shapes which have a red dot.

God led his people through the desert for many years. He gave them water from a rock. He gave them quail and sweet manna to eat.

One day Moses went up Mount Sinai to meet God. Moses came down with ten rules to help them to live together happily. The rules were about loving God and loving other people too.

### ✏️ Activity

Put the letter of each picture detail into the numbered grid to show how to rebuild the picture of Moses.

14

# Fed by ravens

### ✏ Activity

Fill in the blanks with the letters 'e' or 'a' to find four things that God sent to keep Elijah alive.

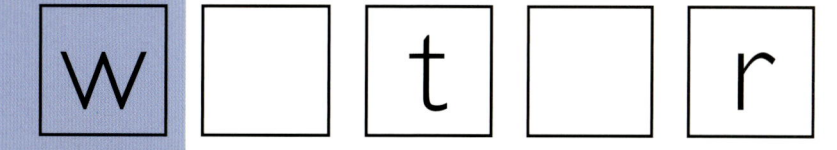

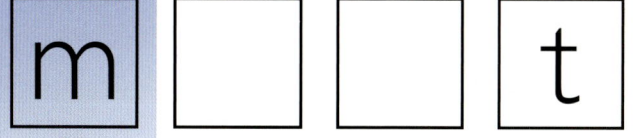

| w |   | t |   | r |   |
|---|---|---|---|---|---|
| r |   | v |   | n | s |
| b | r |   |   | d |   |
| m |   |   | t |   |   |

King Ahab was a bad king. God sent Elijah to tell him no rain would fall until the king kept God's ten rules. The king was very angry so Elijah ran away!

God sent Elijah to a brook with cool, clear water to drink. God sent ravens with food for Elijah to eat.

15

# God takes care of Elijah

When the stream dried up, God sent Elijah to a woman who shared her last meal with Elijah and her son. But when she looked in her jar, there was just enough flour and just enough oil for one more meal. For as long as she shared what she had, there was just enough to feed them until the rain fell again.

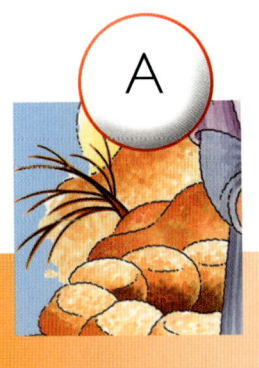

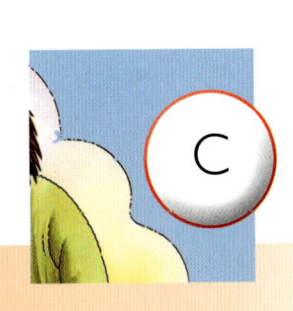

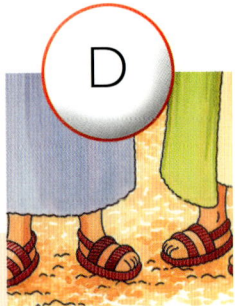

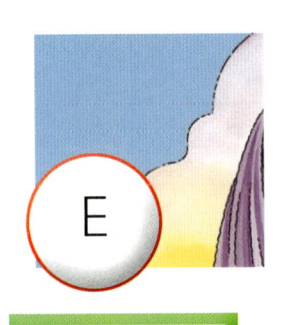

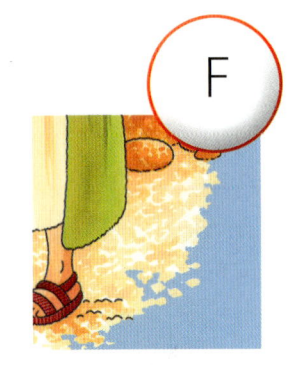

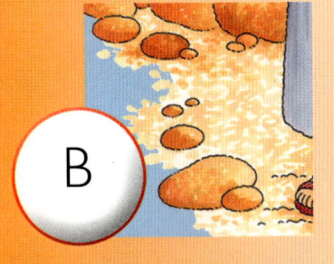

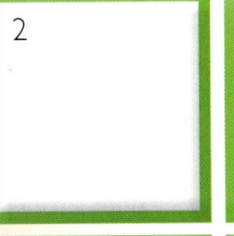

## ✏️ Activity

Write the letter of each picture detail into the grid to show how to rebuild the picture above.

| 1 | 2 | 3 |
|---|---|---|
| 4 | 5 | 6 |
| 7 | 8 | 9 |

16

# Only one God

### ✏️ Activity

Find and circle five things that are wrong with this picture.

### ✏️ Activity

How many people are wearing blue in this picture?

How many people are there in the picture altogether?

Elijah went back to the bad king three years later. Now King Ahab was VERY angry. But he agreed to a contest between God and the gods of wood and stone he and his wife loved.

Ahab's gods could not bring fire down on the altar but when Elijah prayed, God sent down fire! Then all the people worshipped God and knew that he was the only true and living God. Then God sent rain again to the earth.

17

# Jesus is born

Mary and Joseph went to Bethlehem for a census just before Jesus was born. When Mary had her baby, she made a bed for him in the manger because there was no room at the inn.

Then some shepherds came to visit him! They had been told by angels that God's son, the Saviour of the world, had been born.

Later wise men from the east followed a star so they could come to worship the baby king. They gave him gifts of gold, frankincense and myrrh.

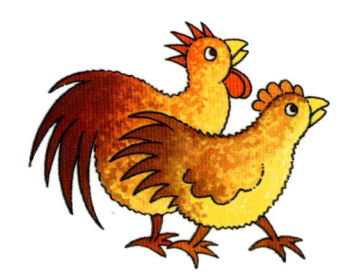

## Activity

Do you know which of these creatures eat hay from a manger? Put a tick (✓) next to them.

- ☐ Ox
- ☐ Snake
- ☐ Chicken
- ☐ Dog
- ☐ Hedgehog
- ☐ Horse

# John baptizes Jesus

When Jesus was a man, he went down to the River Jordan where John was baptizing people. Jesus asked to be baptized too.

John knew who Jesus was.

'I can't,' John said. 'For everyone else baptism is a sign that God forgives your sins – but you have done nothing wrong. You should be baptizing me!'

But Jesus asked John again. As he came up from under the water, the people saw a dove over the water. The Holy Spirit blessed Jesus and they heard God's voice.

'This is my son. He has made me very happy today.'

### Activity

Who did God say Jesus was?

This is my...

### Activity

Find six differences between the two pictures and draw a circle round them.

# Jesus makes friends

Jesus knew that God wanted him to show people how much God loved them. He chose twelve men to be his friends and help him as he travelled about teaching the people.

Some of them were fishermen like brothers Peter and Andrew, James and John. Matthew collected taxes for the Romans. James and Jude were also brothers. Philip, Bartholomew, Simon, Thomas and Judas Iscariot were the other disciples.

## Activity

How many special friends did Jesus choose?

## Activity

One friend of Jesus had been a tax collector. How many coins can you see below?

# Don't worry

## ✏️ Activity

Tick (✓) the picture that is the odd one out.

1
2
3

Jesus told people that God loved them and would take care of them.

'Don't worry about what you will eat or what you will wear,' he said. 'Look at the birds – God feeds them all. Look at the flowers – what could be more beautiful! God loves you more than the birds and the flowers – he will take care of you. Try to live God's way, and he will make sure you have everything you need.'

## ✏️ Activity

Circle the three mistakes in the text below.

Jesus said: God loves you more than the birds and the moon – he will take pictures of you. Try to live God's way, and he will make sure you have something you need.'

21

# The man on the mat

There was a man in Capernaum who couldn't walk. Four of his friends carried him on his mat to the house where Jesus was teaching. But so many people had gathered to listen that there was no room.

The friends carried him up the outside steps – and started to make a hole in the roof! They lowered their friend down to the place where Jesus was and Jesus healed him! The man was able to carry his mat home!

## Activity

Can you find the way to Jesus?

# The storm on the lake

Jesus had been teaching and healing people all day and he was very tired. He fell asleep as soon as he felt the waves lapping gently against the side of the boat as his friends sailed him across Lake Galilee.

Suddenly the gentle breeze became a storm that rocked the boat violently. Water sloshed over the sides and the disciples were afraid they would drown!

They woke Jesus. He stood and spoke to the wind and waves – and Lake Galilee became calm again. The disciples were amazed. How did Jesus do that?

## ✏ Activity

Complete the picture by tracing over the grey lines.

# Miracle on the mountain

✏️ **Activity**

Make a copy of the fish in the lower box.

It was evening and a huge crowd of more than 5000 people were with Jesus, far from their homes. Jesus wanted to give them something to eat.

Andrew brought a boy to Jesus who had two little fish and five pieces of bread he was willing to share. Jesus thanked the boy and thanked God and then shared the food with his disciples who then shared it with the people in the crowd. Everyone had enough to eat – and there were even twelve baskets of leftovers. God had blessed them.

✏️ **Activity**

Write the name of the disciple who brought the boy to Jesus in the box below.

# The Lost Sheep

Jesus once told a story about a shepherd who had 100 sheep. When he counted them he found that one was missing. So he left the 99 and went to search for the one that was missing.

When he found it, he brought it home, happy that he had found his one missing sheep.

Jesus said that God was like that shepherd – he cared about even one person who was lost and alone.

## Activity

Track the path to the lost sheep without touching the green edges.

25

# Be kind to others

Jesus told this story to a man who wanted to know how to please God.

'A man was attacked on his way from Jerusalem to Jericho. As he lay wounded and dying in the heat of the day, a priest walked by. Later another religious man came along – but he also walked by. Then a man from Samaria stopped. He cleaned and bandaged the man's wounds and helped him onto his own donkey. He took him to an inn and paid for him to be cared for till he was well again.

'You will please God if you act in the same way as the Good Samaritan,' said Jesus.

## Activity

Starting here, find your way through the maze to Jericho.

# The man who climbed a tree

Zacchaeus was a rich tax collector who cheated people. He had no friends. So when Jesus came to Jericho, Zacchaeus wanted so much to see him that he climbed a tree to get a good look!

As Zacchaeus looked down on Jesus, Jesus looked up and spoke to him. 'I'd like to come to your house today, Zacchaeus.'

Zacchaeus was so happy that he scrambled down the tree. Jesus was his friend! And from that day he became a kind and generous man. He paid back the people he had cheated and gave lots of money to the poor.

## Activity

Find and circle ten differences between these two pictures.

# The last supper

### Activity
Which face is not in the picture below?

A  B
C  D

When Jesus and his disciples went to Jerusalem to celebrate Passover, people waved and cheered.

'Hooray!' the people shouted. 'It's Jesus, our king!'

But a few days later, as they sat down to eat supper together, Jesus seemed thoughtful. As he shared the bread with his friends, he told them it was his body, broken for them. As he offered them the cup of red wine to share, he described it as his blood, shed for them.

Jesus had many friends but he had made enemies among the Jewish religious leaders. They were plotting his death.

### Activity

Fill in the missing word.

Jesus said the broken bread was like his body. He said his blood was represented by ...

___  ___  ___   ___  ___  ___  ___

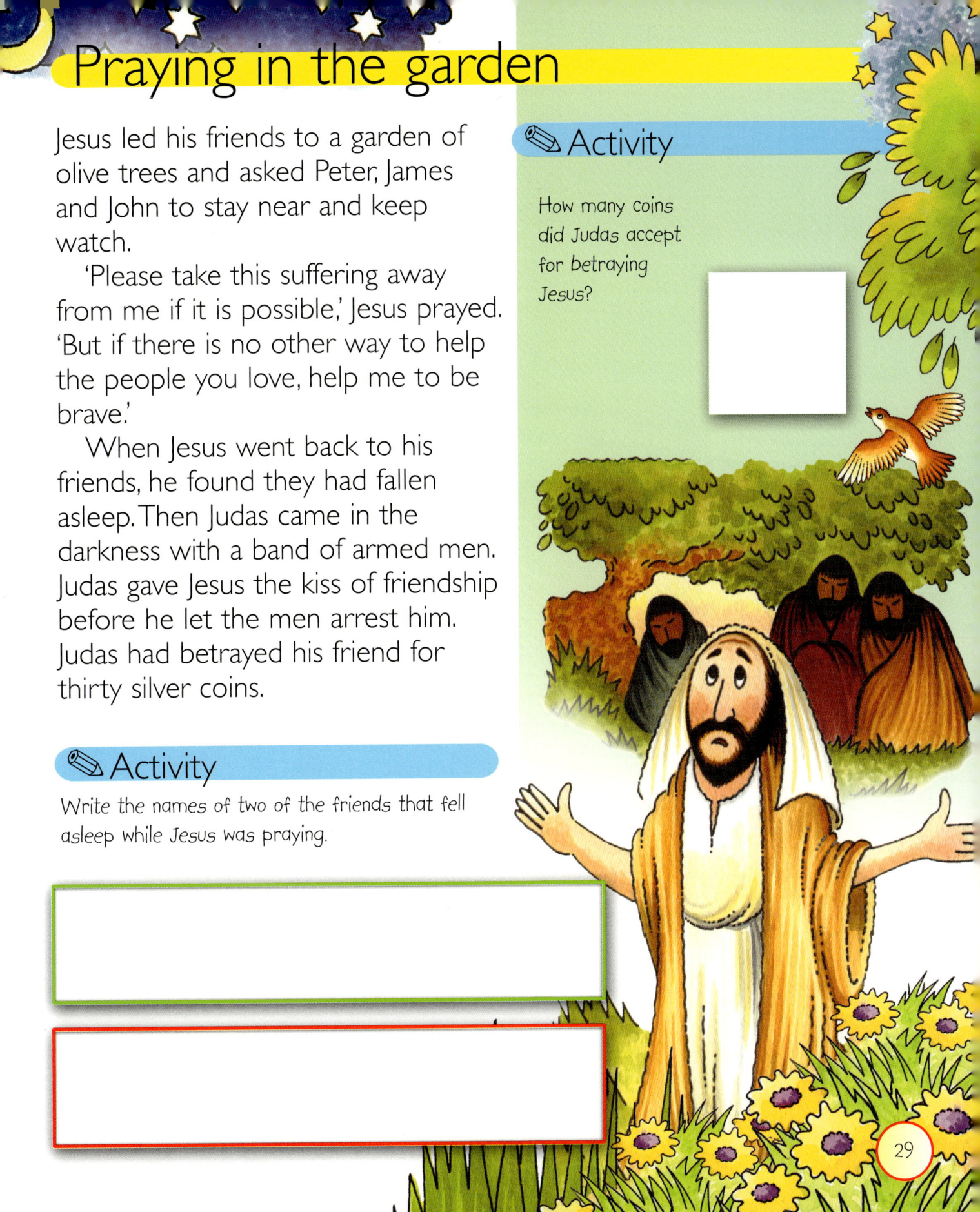

# Praying in the garden

Jesus led his friends to a garden of olive trees and asked Peter, James and John to stay near and keep watch.

'Please take this suffering away from me if it is possible,' Jesus prayed. 'But if there is no other way to help the people you love, help me to be brave.'

When Jesus went back to his friends, he found they had fallen asleep. Then Judas came in the darkness with a band of armed men. Judas gave Jesus the kiss of friendship before he let the men arrest him. Judas had betrayed his friend for thirty silver coins.

## ✏ Activity

How many coins did Judas accept for betraying Jesus?

## ✏ Activity

Write the names of two of the friends that fell asleep while Jesus was praying.

29

# Jesus dies on a cross

Jesus was not found guilty of any crime but he was taken by soldiers to a hill called Golgotha and crucified by the Romans between two thieves.

All the disciples had run away and hidden except for John who stood with Mary, the mother of Jesus, at the foot of the cross.

After Jesus had died, he was taken down and buried in the tomb of a man called Joseph from Arimathea.

## Activity

How many crosses were there on the hillside?

## Activity

Tick (✓) the five soldiers that are exactly the same.

A   B   C   D

E   F   G   H

# Jesus is alive!

Jesus died on a Friday. Early on Sunday morning women went to the garden where they had seen Jesus buried. But the stone door had been rolled away – and the tomb was empty.

Mary Magdalene stood weeping. Then Jesus stood beside her and spoke her name. Mary was the first of many people to see that Jesus was very much alive. God had raised him from death!

## Activity

Track the way to the tomb without touching the edges of the path.

## Activity

Tick (✓) the answers here that are correct. Put a cross (✗) next to those that are wrong.

1. ☐ Jesus died on a Friday.

2. ☐ The women went to the tomb on Monday.

3. ☐ The window of the tomb was open.

4. ☐ The tomb was empty.

5. ☐ Jesus was alive.

# ANSWERS

**Page 2**
1 axe, 2 ladder, 3 brush

**Page 3**
1 frog, 2 zebra, 3 giraffe, 4 crocodile or alligator

**Page 4**
1 lion, 2 tiger, 3 leopard

**Page 5**
1 red, 2 orange, 3 yellow, 4 green, 5 blue

**Page 6**
1 green, 2 orange, 3 purple

**Page 7**

**Page 8**
1 B baker, 2 S shepherd, 3 W wine steward

**Page 9**

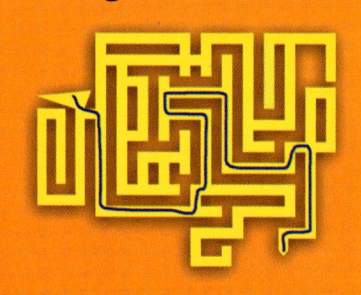

**Page 10**

**Page 11**
There are 6 frogs

Shoe D

**Page 12**
1 ✓, 2 ✓, 3 ✗, 4 ✗, 5 ✓, 6 ✓, 7 ✓, 8 ✓, 9 ✗

**Page 13**
1 C, 2 E, 3 A, 4 ✗, 5 F, 6 B, 7 D, 8 G

**Page 14**

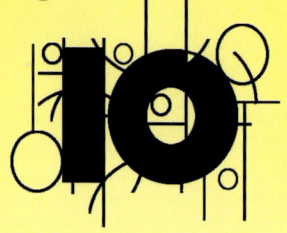

1:A, 2:C, 3:E, 4:D, 5:G, 6:F, 7:B, 8: H

**Page 15**
water, ravens, bread, meat

**Page 16**
1 E, 2 H, 3 C, 4 A, 5 G, 6 I, 7 B, 8 D, 9 F

**Page 17**

**Page 17**
4 people are wearing blue; there are 11 people altogether

**Page 18**
Ox ✓ horse ✓

**Page 19**
God said that Jesus was his son.

**Page 20**
12

11

**Page 21**
2

Jesus said: God loves you more than the birds and the (moon) – he will take (pictures) of you. Try to live God's way, and he will make sure you have (something) you need.'

**Page 22**

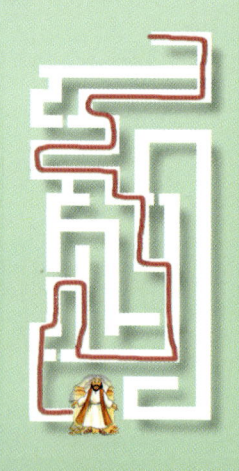

**Page 24**
Andrew

**Page 26**

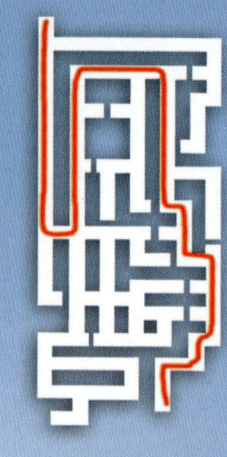

**Page 27**

**Page 28**
D

red wine

**Page 29:**
30

Peter, James or John

**Page 30:**
3

A, C, D, E, G

**Page 31:**
1 ✓, 2 ✗, 3 ✗, 4 ✓, 5 ✓